... THE STARS

– The Story of the Snowdon Mountain Railway

THE WAY TO THE STARS
- THE STORY OF THE
SNOWDON MOUNTAIN RAILWAY

Keith Turner

ISBN: 0-86381-954-0

Cover design: Sian Parri

First published in 2005 by
Gwasg Carreg Gwalch, 12 Iard yr Orsaf, Llanrwst, Wales LL26 0EH
Tel: 01492 642031   Fax: 01492 641502
e-mail: books@carreg-gwalch.co.uk   website: www.carreg-gwalch.co.uk

ACKNOWLEDGEMENTS

I should like to express my thanks to all those individuals, companies, institutions, libraries and individuals in Wales and England who, over many years, have assisted me in a variety of ways with my researches into the history of this most fascinating of railways, not least by allowing me to include their photographs in this book. A special debt of gratitude is owed to all those Snowdon Mountain Railway staff, past and present, who have answered so patiently all requests for information during my visits to the line.

CONTENTS

Sic itur ad astra

('Such is the way to the stars')

The motto of the original
Snowdon Mountain Tramroad & Hotels Co Ltd.

The logo of the new Snowdon Mountain Railway Ltd as used on a pre-World War II publicity leaflet.

GLOSSARY OF
WELSH PLACE-NAMES

For the benefit of non-Welsh speakers, a brief glossary of the more important Welsh place-names and place-name elements used in this book, follows.

Afon – River
Ceunant Mawr – Great Ravine
Clogwyn – Cliff or precipice
Clogwyn du'r Arddu – Black Cliff
Eryri – Abode of Eagles; or High Land. The terms arise from different derivations of the word
Llan – Church; hence village. Llanberis is named after St Peris, a semi-legendary Welsh or Roman anchorite who had a cell here
Llyn – Lake
Moel – Hill or mountain
Nant – Brook; gorge
Rhyd-ddu – Black Ford
Yr Wyddfa – The Grave or Burial Place. Traditionally the grave of the ancient giant Rhita Gawr

The way to the stars. (Sugden of Llanberis postcard, Author's Collection)

CHRONOLOGY OF MAJOR EVENTS

1639	First recorded ascent of Snowdon, by Thomas Johnson.
1811	First patent for a rack railway, taken out in Britain by John Blenkinsop.
1820	First shelter appeared at the summit of Snowdon.
1827	Cairn erected at the summit of Snowdon by Ordnance Survey team.
1830	Paved road opened through Llanberis Pass.
1863	Rack system specially designed for mountain railways patented, in Paris, by Niklaus Riggenbach.
1868	First section of the world's first mountain rack railway opened in the USA.
1869	London & North Western Railway branch from Caernarfon to Llanberis opened.
1871	First European mountain rack railway opened, up Mount Rigi in Switzerland.
1872	Snowdon Railway Bill introduced, and defeated, in Parliament.
1874	Second unsuccessful Snowdon Railway Bill.
1877	Third proposal for a Snowdon railway, this time by J.S. Hughes and C.E. Spooner of the Festiniog Railway.
1880s	Llanberis hit by economic slump.
1881	North Wales Narrow Gauge Railways tourist line to Snowdon opened.
1894	Syndicate formed to promote the case for a rack railway up Snowdon.
1896	The Snowdon railway opened - and closed - by the Snowdon Mountain Tramroad & Hotels Co Ltd.
1897	The railway reopens.
1928	Company name changed to the Snowdon Mountain Railway Ltd.
1986	Diesel locomotives introduced to supplement the steam engines.
1995	Diesel railcars introduced.
1996	Centenary of the railway's opening.
2004	Permission granted for a totally new Summit building, and for a visitors' theatre at Llanberis Station.

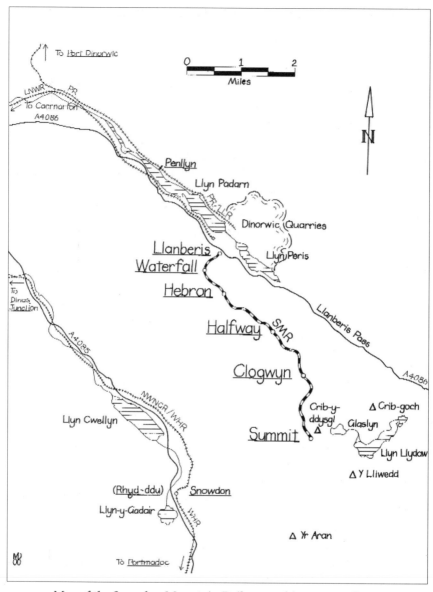

Map of the Snowdon Mountain Railway and its surroundings,
including the Padarn Railway (closed 1961), the LNWR/BR branch from
Caernarfon (closed 1962) and, on the other side of the mountain,
the North Wales Narrow Gauge Railways/Welsh Highland Railway
(closed 1936 but currently being reopened in stages).

Introduction

The only railway of its type in the British Isles, the Snowdon Mountain Railway has long been justly famous for its unique features appealing to railway enthusiast and holidaymaker alike. To begin with, it is a rack railway and as such tackles gradients as steep as 1 in 5½ as it climbs more than 3,100ft in less than 5 miles. Secondly, for over a century it boasted the highest railway station in Britain: Summit Station at 3,493ft above sea level. (This title was lost only in December 2001 when the CairnGorm Mountain Railway opened, near Aviemore in Scotland, replacing a skiers' chairlift; its upper terminus is some 100ft higher than that of the SMR.) Finally, although diesel traction was introduced in 1986, the railway still employs steam locomotives to propel its carriages up the highest mountain in Wales, as it has done ever since it opened in 1896.

Owned by a private company, the railway is not a 'preserved line' like so many of Wales' other narrow gauge railways, but has always been a commercial venture in its own right. Long may it continue to delight, intrigue and enthrall all those who come to view - and ride on - this engineering marvel of a bygone age.

A Brief History of the Snowdon Mountain Railway

Snowdon

In late medieval times the name Snowdon - literally the 'Mountain of Snow' - was applied broadly to the whole region of north-west Wales known today as Snowdonia. This was because the area was poorly served by road - or even track - and was therefore seldom seen by the English except from a distance. The modern usage of the name is both for its horseshoe-shaped chain of peaks together with the outlying Yr Aran to the south, and for the central, highest peak of all - all commonly being regarded as one. Snowdon is of course the English appellation; for the Welsh the matter is more precisely defined. The whole massif is termed Eryri ('Abode of Eagles', or simply 'High Land') and the individual peaks are Yr Aran (2,451ft), Y Lliwedd (2,947ft), Crib-goch (3,023ft), Crib-y-ddysgl (3,496ft) and Yr Wyddfa which, rising to a height of 3,560ft above sea level, makes Snowdon the highest land-mass in Britain south of the Scottish border.

The first recorded ascent of the mountain took place in 1639 and was made by Thomas Johnson, a botanist - the first (or one of the very first) in a long line of travellers to reach the summit in the interests of science. For the casual traveller at that time, however, not only was the ascent of Snowdon an arduous and hazardous one, so was the journey to reach the mountain in the first place and it was another two centuries before that situation was to change.

A Valentine's Series postcard of the summit of Snowdon immediately prior to the construction of the railway, showing the two methods of ascent available to tourists: on foot or on horseback. (Author's Collection)

The summit cairn on another Valentine's postcard, this time of a somewhat later date. The young man on the left appears to be using a new-fangled box camera to take his friend's photograph. (Author's Collection)

THE TOURIST BOOM

It was not until 1830 that a road, replacing the previous steep and rocky path, was made in the very shadow of the mountain through Llanberis Pass, so providing a link between Caernarfon and Capel Curig and, from there, England; such was its effect that by the very next year the ascent of Snowdon was noted as being one of the principal attractions of the area. For many of those who made the journey, the long climb commenced at Llanberis for from there began the lengthiest, but gentlest, of all the paths up the mountain.

At the beginning of the nineteenth century the summit of Snowdon - or Yr Wyddfa - was a flatish space nearly 50ft in circumference, surrounded by a low wall of unknown origin. By 1805 a small cairn had appeared, presumably built from the collected stones of climbers, and about 1820 the wall was dismantled to provide construction material for a small hut 30ft below the summit, the first in a long series of shelters and (from the 1830s) refreshment huts maintained by the professional mountain guides operating, until the coming of the railway, mainly from Llanberis and Beddgelert, hired by visitors to lead them safely up - and down - the mountain.

In 1827 the mountain played an important part in the Ordnance Survey mapping of Great Britain. Trigonometric methods were used with the largest triangle employed being formed by Snowdon, Slieve Donard in Ulster and Scafell Pike in Cumberland; to mark the exact spot sighted a large cairn and trig point, of the type familiar to countless walkers and climbers, were erected. The present cairn on Snowdon dates from this time and does not, as popular legend has it, mark the grave of an ancient giant, though possibly the legend is based on some foundation of truth as the ancient name of Yr Wyddfa ('The Burial Place') implies.

On 1 July 1869 came a branch of the London & North Western Railway from Caernarfon eastwards to Llanberis; the summit of Snowdon was now only five miles from the nearest railhead, and the little village of Llanberis was fairly and squarely on the tourist map.

The approach to Llanberis from the south: a Dennis & Sons postcard of Llanberis Pass and its winding road. (Author's Collection)

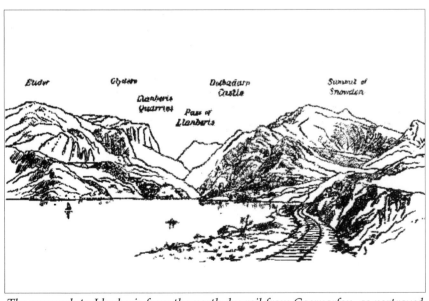

The approach to Llanberis from the north: by rail from Caernarfon, as portrayed in a pre-World War I Gossipping Guide to Wales.

THE STORY OF THE RACK

The Snowdon Mountain Railway is a rack railway. That is to say, it relies for its effectiveness not on the adhesion between wheels and rails as on a conventional railway, but on the meshing of cogs or pinions on the locomotives and a toothed rack rail laid flush with the running rails; by this means the engines can haul themselves up slopes far steeper than a conventional railway could ever tackle. This ingenious principle was patented as early as 1811, when the use of locomotives on railways was still very much in its infancy, by the Manager of Middleton Colliery in Yorkshire, John Blenkinsop. His rack consisted of vertically-set hollow teeth cast as part of the outer side of one of the two cast iron running rails, these engaging with a large pinion-wheel attached to the side of a locomotive and driven round by it.

Thus the world's first rack railway was born. Using steam locomotives, the Middleton line operated as a rack railway until the middle of the nineteenth century, by which time the idea had been tried elsewhere in Britain but abandoned, its one great asset ignored: the ability to overcome gradients far too steep for normal adhesion working. That asset, however, was recognized in other countries and in 1867-69 the first rack mountain railway of the type we know today was constructed up Mount Washington in New Hampshire, USA, by an entrepreneur named Sylvester Marsh. It utilised a centrally-mounted rack assembly shaped much like a ladder laid flat and was quickly followed, in 1871, by a similar one up Mount Rigi in Switzerland built by Niklaus Riggenbach, a Swiss locomotive engineer; so successful were these two railways as tourist attractions that others soon sprang up thick and fast around the world.

An early Valentine's postcard of the approach to Summit Station. The main focus of attention is on the track, which would have been of great interest to visitors as an intriguing novelty. The two, staggered rack blades and their guard rails are centred between the running rails, all being bolted to hollow steel sleepers. At only a very few locations - including points and in Llanberis Station and yard - one of the rack blades, and both the guard rails, are dispensed with. (Courtesy Jan Dobrzynski)

Pointwork in Llanberis Station. Not only do sections of the running rails move, so do sections of the rack blades to ensure an unbroken contact with a locomotive's pinions when it is taking either road through the point. (Jan Dobrzynski)

EARLY PROPOSALS

In the very same year that the Rigi mountain railway was opened, a group of promoters proposed the construction of a rack line from Llanberis to a point nearly half a mile from the summit of Snowdon. The proposal came hot on the heels of the immediate success of Riggenbach's venture and a Bill to authorise the railway's construction was presented to Parliament in 1872. According to its accompanying plans, the line was to commence opposite the LNWR station in Llanberis and, after a short stretch on the level, was to climb the northern flank of Snowdon for just over 4 miles (closely following the path from Llanberis) to a terminus about 500ft below the summit; gradients would have been as severe as 1 in 4 - dangerously steep for a Riggenbach-type line. The promoters of the Bill however, faced with the insurmountable obstacle of non-cooperation on the part of the very influential local landowner, and on the part of his tenants, were soon forced to abandon their project and admit defeat.

A second attempt to build a railway up Snowdon was made in November 1874 when a second Bill, for a similar line, was deposited, only for it to meet with a similar fate. The idea of such a railway then lay dormant until 1877 when it was revived by two men closely connected with the operation of the nearby narrow gauge Ffestiniog Railway, J.S.Hughes and C.E. Spooner, who proposed building a rack railway from Llanberis up one side of the mountain and down the other to meet up with the North Wales Narrow Gauge Railways' line from Dinas Junction, near Caernarfon, to Snowdon Station (opened 1881). Their plan was in fact but one part of a grandiose scheme covering the principal peaks of the British Isles - but it too progressed no further than being a pipe dream.

A TRIP TO
SNOWDON

BY THE NORTH WALES NARROW GAUGE (2 FT.) OR
"TOY" RAILWAY

Which forms a Junction with the L. & N. W. Railway

AT DINAS,

THREE MILES SOUTH OF CARNARVON.

SHORTEST AND MOST
PICTURESQUE ROUTE.

TOURIST TICKETS

(1st and 3rd Class) for Two Calendar Months, renewable up to 31st December, are issued from MAY 1st to October 21st at the **principal** stations in the United Kingdom to **SNOWDON** Station.

Holders of these tickets can break the journey at Rhyl, Llandudno, and other North Wales Pleasure Resorts, completing the outward journey any fine day, visiting Beddgelert, Gelert's Grave, the noted Pass of Aberglaslyn, and other places of interest, or they can "do" SNOWDON.

Conveyances for Beddgelert meet all trains at Snowdon Station and passengers should secure Cheap Return Coach Tickets at that Station.

Cheap Excursion Tickets

will be issued during the season, June 1st to September 30th (certain days excepted), from Rhyl, Llandudno, and all other stations on the Chester and Holyhead Section, to Snowdon (late Rhyd-ddu) Station.

For full details as to fares, times, &c., see bills issued by L. & N. W. and North Wales Narrow Gauge Railway Companies, or apply to—

S. TANNER,

Secretary and Traffic Manager.

DINAS STATION, near CARNARVON.

An advertisement for the North Wales Narrow Gauge Railways' line to Snowdon, as printed in Ward, Lock & Co's 1896 Pictorial and Descriptive Guide to North Wales. *Until the opening of the rack railway on the other side of the mountain this line posed a serious threat to Llanberis' tourist trade and was extended (as the Welsh Highland Railway) to Porthmadog in 1923.*

OPPOSITION

In the 1870s much of Snowdon formed part of the extensive Vaynol Estate, stretching northwards as far as the Menai Strait and in the ownership of George William Duff Assheton-Smith. His influence was great and any scheme to lay a railway up his mountain needed his support; in the case of the above-mentioned Bills, this support was not forthcoming as he simply did not regard the idea as being in his own, or possibly Llanberis', best interests. Also in his ownership was the vast complex of slate quarries across Llyn Padarn from Llanberis known collectively as the Dinorwic Quarries, linked to the Menai Strait by the 4ft gauge Padarn Railway. The principal source of employment for the people of Llanberis and the surrounding area, as the quarries prospered, so did the village.

The slate trade boomed in the years 1863-66, giving birth to yet more quarries in the district. In 1871 the population of Llanberis was 2,507 and fast approaching a peak of 3,033 ten years later; now served by rail, the village was cashing in on the tourist boom as well with its hotels, guest houses and mountain guides.

This then was the background to Assheton-Smith's opposition. Far from being opposed to railways in general, he was fully aware of their precise value. The slate boom had brought prosperity to Llanberis and since the coming of the LNWR branch the village was enjoying an ever-increasing flow of summer tourists; there simply seemed little call for a line up Snowdon. Furthermore, Assheton-Smith's voice was by no means the only one raised against the idea: for some the railway would be an ugly marring of the beauty of the mountain, whilst for others the idea meant that the need for mountain guides and ponies would disappear, and guest houses would lose their trade, as visitors could arrive by train from the surrounding seaside resorts, 'do' Snowdon by rail and be gone, all in the same day.

One is tempted to quote the words of an old Welsh proverb: 'It is easy to say "Yonder is Snowdon", but not so easy to ascend it.' But things were about to change.

Dr Roman S. Abt, the Swiss engineer whose particular improved rack design - patented in 1882 - was the one adopted for use on the Snowdon Mountain Railway. (Courtesy SMR)

THE SMT&H CO LTD

The 1880s were marked by a building depression accompanied by an over-production of slate in Wales, strong competition from other materials and a growing use of cheaper imported slate. The golden days were over and the crash spelt economic disaster for Llanberis; although the industry did slowly revitalise, it was as but a shadow of its former self.

Once again attention was turned to the commercial possibilities of Snowdon - especially the possibility of a railway to the summit. European examples were held up for examination and found to be attractive and, as the 1890s progressed and the general prosperity of the village declined, pressure steadily mounted for such a line to be built from Llanberis. Early in 1894 Assheton-Smith's Estate Agent, Captain N.P. Stewart, formed a syndicate of local and Liverpool interests to promote the case for a mountain railway - this time privately rather than adopting the risky procedure of promoting yet another Bill in Parliament. It was felt that this way would have a far greater chance of success, and that judgement was soon proved to be sound: realising that the scheme would almost certainly be the salvation of the village, Assheton-Smith gave his wholehearted support to the new plan, having ascertained - through Stewart - that the project now had the backing of the local populace in general and his tenants in particular.

The next step was to form the necessary commercial body for the undertaking and accordingly, on 16 November 1894, the Snowdon Mountain Tramroad & Hotels Co Ltd was formally registered, holding its first meeting in the Queen's Hotel in Chester. Its stated aim was 'To construct a tramroad from Llanberis, in the County of Caernarvon, to a point at or near the summit of Snowdon, in the parish of Beddgelert, in the same county, and to erect an hotel at or near the summit.' Together with the lease of the Royal Victoria Hotel in Llanberis, this meant that soon the Company would, in effect, be running two hotels linked by a railway - one at the foot and the other at the summit of the highest mountain in Wales!

THE

Snowdon Mountain Tramroad and Hotels Company

LIMITED.

(Incorporated under the Companies Acts, 1862 to 1890.)

CAPITAL - - - - £70,000.

Divided into 7,000 Shares of £10 each.

Issue of 6,343 Shares of £10 each—and £20,000, part of an issue of £35,000 Four and a Half per Cent. First Mortgage Debentures of £100 each.

The Debentures will constitute a first charge upon the entire undertaking and property of the Company. They will be for 20 years, but redeemable at the option of the Company after the 1st July, 1905, upon 6 months' notice.

The Interest on the Debentures will be payable Half-Yearly, on 1st January and 1st July in each year.

FIRST MORTGAGE DEBENTURES	SHARES.
Payable £10 per £100 on Application.	Payable 10/- per Share on Application.
£40 „ „ Allotment.	£1 10/- „ „ Allotment
£50 „ „ 1st Jan., 1896.	£3 „ „ 1st Aug., 1895.
	Balance in calls not exceeding £2 per Share and at intervals of not less than two months.

Allottees may, however, pay up in full on Allotment. Dividend and Interest being payable on the Shares and Debentures from dates of payment.

DIRECTORS.

J. S. HARMOOD BANNER, Esq., 24, North John Street, Liverpool, Chartered Accountant.
HARRY CLEGG, Esq., Plas Llanfair, Anglesea.
Lt.-Col. WALLACE W. CRAGG, Southelms, Shortlands, Kent.
R. E. L. NAYLOR, Esq., 17, King Street, Liverpool, Banker.
Lord ALEXANDER PAGET, Plas Newydd, Anglesea.
Capt. N. P. STEWART, Bryntirion, Port Dinorwic.
F. W. TURNER, Esq., Plas Brereton, Carnarvon.

BANKERS.

LEYLAND & BULLINS, 11, Dale Street, Liverpool.
WILLIAMS & CO., Old Bank, Chester, and their Branches, and as their Agents—
ROBARTS, LUBBOCK & CO., 15, Lombard Street, London, E.C.
Solicitors—WALTER WEBB & CO., 23, Queen Victoria Street, London, E.C.
Engineers—Sir DOUGLAS FOX & FRANCIS FOX, 28, Victoria Street, Westminster, S.W.
Architects—F. & G. HOLME, Crosshall Street, Liverpool.
Secretary and Manager—G. C. AITCHISON.
Registered Office—VICTORIA HOTEL, LLANBERIS.
Temporary London Office—28, VICTORIA STREET, WESTMINSTER, S.W.

An 1895 advertisement inviting investors to purchase shares in the SMT&H Co Ltd. Note the vignette top right giving an artist's very grandiose impression of the proposed Summit Hotel - quite unlike what was later built!

CONSTRUCTION

Things were now moving fast. The route that the railway was to take had already been surveyed and engineers and contractors were now appointed, and track, two steam locomotives and four bogie coaches ordered (with all the stock constructed to designs similar to those in use on other European rack railways); the gauge chosen for the line was 800mm, or nominally 2ft 7½ in. Everything was now ready for the actual task of construction to begin.

On Saturday 15 December 1894 the first sod of the railway was ceremoniously cut by Assheton-Smith's six-year-old daughter Enid. Work then began immediately on the construction of the line, starting at Llanberis with both earthworks and track-laying, and so progressing on up the mountain, using the portion so far completed to transport men, materials and equipment to the ever-advancing railhead where the workers were housed in temporary huts. (This plan also meant that after the winter, as the line climbed higher, so the weather would improve.) By April 1895 a total of over 200 men were being employed on the construction of the railway and the average rate of track laying was 120yd per day; the record was 350yd. The particular rack assembly used was of a design invented by Roman Abt, an employee of Riggenbach's; this utilized a pair of toothed blades mounted vertically in the centre of the track and was an improvement on the old ladder-type design.

The summit - or rather Summit Station, just below the actual summit of Yr Wyddfa - was reached on 6 January 1896, the final 4½ miles of track having been laid in only 72 working days. It was a remarkable feat in view of the conditions under which the work had had to be carried out, though completion was just over six months behind schedule. Three days later, on Thursday 9 January, the first train arrived at Summit, carrying various officials and representatives of the SMT&H Co Ltd and the contractors. Their dream of a railway to the top of Snowdon had, at long last, become a reality.

Photographs of the Snowdon Mountain Railway under construction are rare and usually of poor quality. One of the better ones is this view of the impressive Afon Hwch Viaduct being built, with one of the locos on a works train.
(Symons of Llanberis)

Track-laying just below the future site of Waterfall Station - the first halt above Llanberis - with a works train in the background. The rack blades are being laid first since they had to be perfectly aligned all the way up the mountain.
(Courtesy SMR)

Opening

During February and March 1896 a number of test trains were run over the railway, carrying invited guests, members of the press and the like; the opening to the public was set for Easter Monday, with all ceremony to be dispensed with and quiet efficiency to be the order of the day. It was to be a disaster.

At 10.50am on 6 April 1896 the first public train steamed out of Llanberis Station on the start of its hour-long ascent, followed shortly by the second. Soon after noon locomotive No 1 *L.A.D.A.S.* (named from the initials of Assheton-Smith's wife, Laura) led the first train down the mountain but, fifteen minutes out from Summit, the train began to run away - only for the two coaches to be halted by the railway's General Manager applying the brake. Two passengers had already leapt from the train though and one, Ellis Roberts, landlord of the Padarn Villa Hotel in Llanberis, died that night of his injuries. As for *L.A.D.A.S.*, she had careered down the embankment, hit a sharp left-hand bend at a fantastic rate of speed and leapt from the rails down a 300ft precipice. The result was her almost total destruction. Luckily, both her driver and fireman had already jumped clear and were virtually unscathed.

Worse was to follow: No 2 *Enid* with the second descending train ploughed into the two (now thankfully empty) coaches of the first train, sending both hurtling down the steep slope towards the next station - Clogwyn - where they toppled onto their sides in the passing loop there.

The expert consensus was that recent snow and ice in the cutting had unsettled the shaly nature of the rock, leading to a slight subsidence of the track. The outcome was the fatal lurch of *L.A.D.A.S.* on the descent when her pinions had slipped off the rack, throwing the locomotive out of control. Strangely, public services were not suspended until the following weekend, after which it was decided to fit guard rails to the rack, and grippers to engage them to the locos, so that such an occurrence could never happen again.

One of the few known photographs of the ill-fated L.A.D.A.S. Here she is just outside Llanberis Station, perhaps on a pre-opening day special working - or possibly even on the morning of the opening day itself. (Courtesy SMR)

Reopening

By the following Easter the task of laying the guard rails was still uncompleted with the final ¼ mile up to Summit remaining to be tackled. Notwithstanding this it was decided to go ahead and reopen the line on the day planned - Easter Monday again - but until the work was finished all passenger services, it was announced, would terminate at Clogwyn. And so, Easter in Llanberis was marked for the second consecutive year by the opening to the public of the Snowdon Mountain Tramroad, the actual date being Monday 19 April 1897, with the first trainload of fare-paying passengers leaving Llanberis in the middle of the morning after a pilot train had been run up and down the mountain to ensure that the line was in a perfect state of readiness. The pattern of 1896 was followed in that any ceremony was conspicuous by its absence and the waiting crowd was instead rewarded with the somewhat anticlimactic sight of the 10.45am Llanberis to Clogwyn train steaming steadily away into the trees and over the Afon Hwch Viaduct.

The winter snow on the higher reaches of the mountain had not yet thawed completely and a regular service to Summit would have been a very dubious proposition even if the task of fitting the guard rails had been finished in time. The weather at Clogwyn was very dull to say the least and the view (or what passed for such) not at all impressive. In spite of this the railway was very well patronised throughout the day and when the final train pulled into Llanberis soon after 5.00pm everyone concerned breathed a huge collective sigh of relief that the occasion had passed off without a single hitch - which, considering the events of just twelve months before, was in itself ample compensation for the dreariness of the day.

The aftermath of the accident: looking down the track, from about where L.A.D.A.S. left the rails, to the overturned carriages in Clogwyn Station. Note the absence of guard rails to the rack. This Valentine's postcard of the scene is typical of many produced pre-World War I recording railway and tramway accidents of the period. (Author's Collection)

THE EARLY YEARS

The railway quickly settled down to a trouble-free pattern of working that did much to dispel the memory of the 1896 disaster, and the installation of the guard rails on the upper section of the line was soon finished. The novelty of this new, lazy method of ascending Snowdon made it an immediate tourist attraction for visitors to the region and in 1897 over 12,000 passengers were carried on the railway - now employing three more locomotives - in its first full season of operation.

During World War I a restricted service was operated, but apart from this the railway was not affected at all. With the post-war years came a welcome upsurge in tourism throughout Britain as a whole and the Company made plans to increase the existing service to meet the increased demand for rides, ordering three new locomotives from the Swiss Locomotive & Machine Co. These were delivered in 1922 (No 6) and 1923 (Nos 7 and 8), after which orders were placed with the Schweizerische Industrie-Gesellschaft of Neuhausen for four semi-open carriages. All four were delivered the following year. The new stud of seven locomotives was deemed large enough to finally end the old, unofficial practice of running two-coach trains on occasion. The era of development was now drawing to a close to make way for a period of consolidation marked, in 1928, by the SMT&H Co Ltd changing its name to the more succinct Snowdon Mountain Railway Ltd, from which title the Snowdon Mountain Tramroad took its new name, thereafter being known officially as the Snowdon Mountain Railway.

During the period 1922-24 the railway added three new locomotives and four new carriages to its stock. The first loco to arrive was No 6 Sir Harmood, *named after Sir Harmood Banner, the first Chairman of the SMT&H Co Ltd, though the name was later changed to* Padarn, *as seen here on a Valentine's postcard. (Courtesy Jan Dobrzynski)*

Official works photograph of one of the new coaches - No 9 - at Neuhausen in Switzerland before dispatch to Wales. (SIG Neuhausen)

Service Suspended

The outbreak of World War II in 1939 had, at first, little noticeable effect upon the railway. It closed for the winter at the beginning of September, with a restricted service commencing the following July running through until the end of September; in 1941 the line again operated from mid-July to the end of September. The war effort finally caught up with the railway in 1942 when the Ministry of Supply carried out some experimental radio work at the summit, though a restricted public service was still operated. (Attendance records for residents at the Summit Hotel were in fact broken with more guests staying there than in any previous season, though this state of affairs was at least partly due to the scientific work in progress.)

The railway's season for 1942 was from Whitsun to the end of September; this was repeated in 1943, mainly to serve as a 'blind' since important radar development work was being undertaken in the Summit Hotel, which had been requisitioned by the Air Ministry and closed to the general public. At the end of that September the railway again closed for the winter but did not reopen for the 1944 season for that year the Summit Hotel passed into the control of the Admiralty and further secret radar work was carried out there. (For a brief spell the hotel was also used by the Army!) This period saw the installation of a large tank there to hold copious amounts of drinking water for in the winter the supply trains often could not run for days at a time.

The railway did not reopen to the public until Friday 4 May 1945. Overall, it had suffered during the war years from lack of proper maintenance as a result of a shortage of both men and materials - during this time the staff had dwindled to a grand total of six: one train crew of driver, fireman and guard, plus two gangers and the General Manager who, somehow, had kept the essential trains going, ferrying passengers, supplies and equipment up the mountain.

Even at the top of Snowdon, there was no escape from thoughts of war. Sent to colleagues in Birmingham on 16 September 1940, this Photochrom postcard gives a fittingly sombre view of the railway. On the back the sender has written: 'Hope all is going well at the office and that Jerry is not paying many visits, as all the news we get here is of London. Have managed to climb Snowdon twice – not by the train – in spite of anything but good weather. On the second occasion we got soaked and had to get the hotel people to let us use their drying rooms.' (Author's Collection)

SERVICE RESUMED

The railway was soon back (or very nearly so) to its pre-war levels of traffic, but heavy expenditure was required urgently to keep the line open and work started on the relaying of a considerable portion of the track - nearly 2½ miles in all. Finding supplies of the right materials was a major problem, though by 1948 most of what was needed had been acquired.

The 1950s and 1960s brought with them, inevitably, other changes in the form of modernisation, resulting in better amenities and conditions for passengers. The first (and probably the most appreciated!) of these was the rebuilding of the coaching stock, converting the old semi-open vehicles into more modern-looking closed carriages. While this was going on a start was made on improving the structure of the Summit Hotel; work on this was begun in 1952 and completed two years later. The hotel was now the only one run by the Company for, after several successive years of poor trading figures, it had disposed of the lease of the Royal Victoria Hotel (which had only reopened after the war at Easter 1946) on the last day of December 1951. This meant that from 1952 onwards the Company ceased to be involved in the hotel business altogether for no overnight guests had used the Summit Hotel since the war as all the sleeping accommodation was required by the increased number of staff employed there.

In 1960 modernisation work commenced at the railway's lower terminus with the enlarging and refitting of the station shop, followed in the next year by the modernisation of the restaurant there, the outcome of it all being an increase in takings at both establishments. Further improvements followed in 1968 with the opening of a new 'piazza' at the Summit Hotel, complete with licensed bar. Despite all these improvements, major changes were still to come and the next thirty years would see the railway transformed in almost every aspect of its operation.

The most noticeable visual change to occur on the railway in the decade or so after World War II was the reconstruction of the carriages and their adoption of a new, brighter livery. This is one of the newly-rebuilt 1895 coaches at Clogwyn... (Courtesy SMR)

... and one of the 1923 coaches, similarly treated, higher up the mountain. Note the vertical front end to the bodywork and the metal box protecting the handbrake wheel, both distinguishing features of the younger carriages in their new guise. (Courtesy Lens of Sutton)

Into a New Century

From 1971 - the 75th anniversary of the opening of the SMR - the railway has had company in Llanberis: a 1ft 11½ in gauge pleasure railway laid on the trackbed of the lakeside section of the old Padarn Railway. Known as the Llanberis Lake Railway, or Rheilffordd Llyn Padarn in Welsh, this was extended in 2003 to a new terminus opposite that of the SMR. It, and the Welsh Slate Museum alongside which it passes in the old Dinorwic Quarries, have both both served to draw more visitors to Llanberis. (A project to reopen the former LNWR branch from Caernarfon, closed by British Railways in 1962, as a 'preserved' line came to nothing.)

As has been the case with virtually every other steam railway in Britain, the SMR has been forced by economic necessity to enter the diesel age. In 1986 it took delivery of two powerful diesel-mechanical locomotives from the Hunslet Engine Co, followed in 1991-92 by a further pair. Although costing nearly a quarter of a million pounds each, they soon proved their worth as stand-ins for steam engines undergoing overhauls, and as traction for trains put on at a moment's notice, so that the railway can always run as many trains as possible when the demand is there.

To supplement the coaching stock similarly, in 1988 a new carriage was added to the fleet. Supplied by East Lancashire Coachbuilders Ltd, this brought the number of passenger vehicles to eight, so increasing to that figure the number of trains that could be operated at any one time; the very next year annual passenger figures broke the 100,000 barrier for the first time. Demand for seats though still far outstripped supply at peak periods and, in 1995, the railway took the bold step of purchasing three diesel-electric railcars. Whether diesel traction ever replaces steam on the railway entirely, only time will tell. The experience of other rack railway operators abroad suggests that there ought always to be a place for steam engines, such is their attraction over and above that offered by the mountain ride itself. Long may they continue to thrive on Snowdon.

*In the 1980s and 1990s the SMR prepared for its second century of existence by introducing diesel traction in the shape of four locomotives and three railcars, all built specifically for the railway. The youngest of the locos is No 12 **George**, seen here at Llanberis in 2000, eight years after its arrival. (Jan Dobrzynski)*

UP THE MOUNTAIN

LLANBERIS

Like the village from which it takes its name, Llanberis Station has changed appreciably over the years, though the basic layout is still virtually that of the original. The first, wooden station buildings have been drastically rebuilt, added to and modernised at various times; in a curious way however the latest brick and glass structures retain the rather continental air of their predecessors. Perhaps this is due to the very obvious presence of the all-important rack between the rails, a Swiss alien in the heart of Snowdonia. The station is sited 353ft above sea-level beside, and end-on to, the A4086 from Caernarfon, and adjoins a shop (for postcards, souvenirs and the like), restaurant and museum display.

Crossing the station forecourt, would-be passengers pass through the booking hall and out onto one of the station's two platforms. These face each other across the two short, dead-end roads via which the trains arrive and depart. Just beyond the end of the platforms the two tracks converge to form the main, single running line of the railway as it begins its long journey up the mountain. Almost immediately, a spur off to the right leads into the station yard and its three shed roads where, until recently, the whole of the railway's rolling-stock had to be stabled. (A goods siding originally existed between the main line and the loco shed but after World War I part of the shed was widened over it to form a one-coach workshop; this was extended the length of the loco shed before World War II and the track removed.) Also in the yard are situated such basic necessities as a coaling stage, fuel and water tanks, and a lifting gantry.

On the other side of the running line from the shed are the most recent additions to the Llanberis track layout: two storage sidings laid in 1995 to accommodate the new railcars (and some coaching stock), there being absolutely no room to have squeezed them in anywhere else.

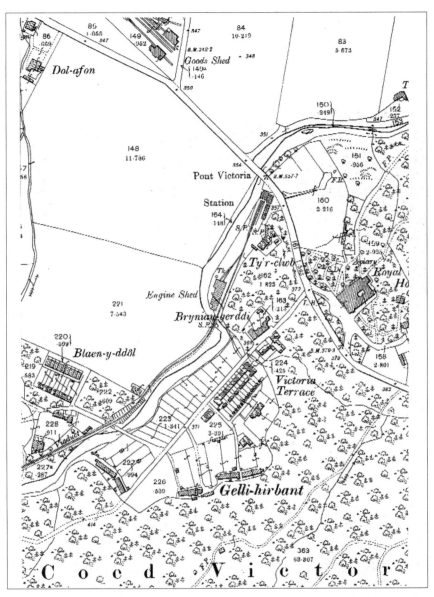

Llanberis Station and the railway to the Afon Hwch Viaduct, as depicted on the 1900 Ordnance Survey 25in to 1 mile map. The track layout in the station - surveyed some time prior to publication - appears not to be completed, lacking as it does the third shed road and the goods siding. At the very top is part of the LNWR station yard and, on the right, the Royal Victoria Hotel.

Llanberis Station, c1920, with a train about ready to depart on its hour-long journey to the summit. (Courtesy SMR)

Llanberis Station seen from the other side of the tracks, with what appears to be the exact same train; the locomotive is No 3, Wyddfa. Driver, fireman and guard pose proudly for the camera. (Courtesy SMR)

The entrance to the station yard at Llanberis. The 'spare' boiler on the right has been removed from one of the engines for overhaul and reuse - possibly on another locomotive - as is common practice on the railway. (Jan Dobrzynski)

No 2 Enid in the shed at Llanberis, 2000. Note the use of a single rack blade here, and the absence of guard rails, to aid access to the underside of the locomotives and carriages. (Jan Dobrzynski)

WATERFALL

At only 1 in 50 the gradient at the Llanberis end of the line is the easiest on the railway but it quickly stiffens to 1 in 6 shortly after leaving the engine shed behind and crossing over to the western bank of the Afon Hwch. This sudden and dramatic increase in the gradient is very apparent to passengers and announces, in no uncertain terms, that the climb up the mountain has begun in earnest. The railway, skirting the edge of the village, now enters the trees and, with the gradient easing to 1 in 8½ , crosses the 500ft-long Afon Hwch Viaduct. Soon the shorter, 190ft Upper Viaduct is reached from which, below the train to the left, can be seen the 60ft drop of the Ceunant Mawr waterfall. Sweeping round to the left the line passes the platform of the former Waterfall Station, officially 41 chains (902yd) out from Llanberis and 597ft above sea-level.

The station site is just inside the boundary of the Snowdonia National Park - established in 1951 with an area of 850 square miles - and from here on the railway remains within the Park's confines. The small, nondescript station building is typical of the intermediate stations: when the railway was built it was expected that they would receive little use so consequently grander structures, and any other passenger amenities, were not provided. The building at Waterfall is now used as a store for permanent way materials. Situated on a gradient of 1 in 20, the station has always had just the single track running through it with no passing loop, though until it was lifted c1905 there was a long goods siding on the western side of the running line.

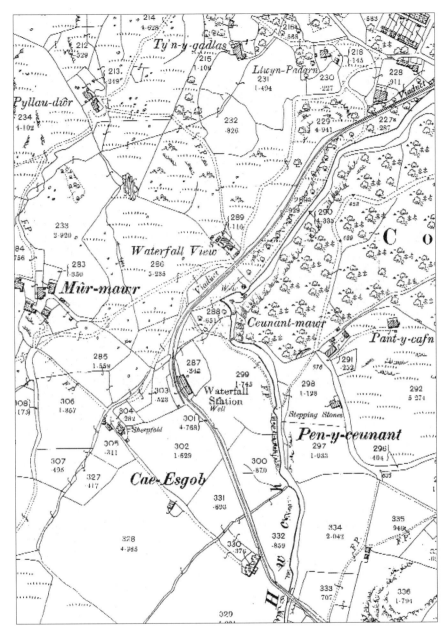

The course of the railway from the Afon Hwch Viaduct to the bridge over the
Afon Hwch south of Waterfall Station, again on the 1900 OS 25in map. Note the
(now lifted) goods siding in the station, intended to serve the neighbouring farms.

43

*Between Llanberis and Waterfall is the most wooded stretch of the railway.
Here, in 2000, diesel locomotive No 12 George takes coach No 8 down off the
Upper Viaduct. (Jan Dobrzynski)*

An original locomotive with an original carriage on the Upper Viaduct, c1930. The lady in the rearmost compartment of the coach is wearing traditional Welsh costume - no doubt for a publicity photo-opportunity of some kind. (Courtesy SMR)

HEBRON

Leaving Waterfall, the railway stretches straight out before the train, climbing like a roller-coaster with its alternate steep and gentle gradients (between 1 in 6 and 1 in 20); in the far distance the summit of Snowdon can be glimpsed on a clear day. The railway has now left the trees and about 260yd out from Waterfall the Afon Hwch is crossed for the second time and after bridging the bridle path from Llanberis to the summit the former Hebron Station is reached, 930ft above sea level.

Originally named Hebron Chapel Station, or simply Chapel Station, after the nearby Calvinist Methodist Capel Hebron, the station is situated on a 1 in 10 slope at a distance of 1 mile 8 chains (1 mile 176yd) from Llanberis. There is a passing loop here which, like all the railway's intermediate loops, is on the right-hand side of the runing line (going up the mountain) having been constructed that way to simplify any later doubling of the track. At the upper end of the loop was originally the railway's third goods siding, just long enough to hold a locomotive and a wagon or two; this was removed in 1920 when hopes of carrying appreciable amounts of freight were abandoned. (The 100yd-long platform here is also testament to the railway planners' optimism - the hoped-for passenger traffic generated by Capel Hebron also never materialised.) There is a water supply here for refilling the steam locomotives but it is rarely used as it is peaty and hence harmful to the engines' boilers; this is a consequence of the marshy nature of the surrounding ground - which has the further disadvantage of being inclined to shrink and subside under the railway, so necessitating constant track inspection and maintenance along this stretch of the line.

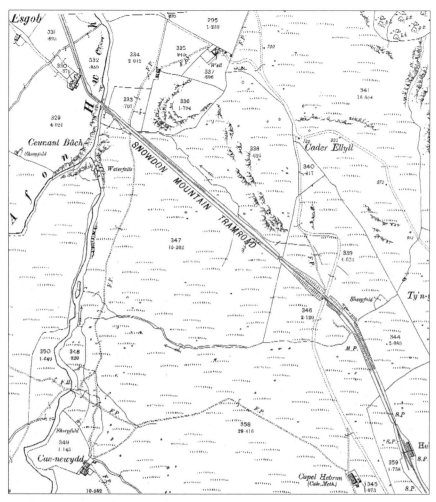

The railway to Hebron Station (and its nearby chapel), again on the 1900 OS 25in map; here is the first passing loop on the line. Note the (now lifted) goods siding and the open moorland that has succeeded the wooded, inhabited lower slopes of the mountain.

After Waterfall the trees are left behind as the railway climbs the next, almost straight stretch of line up to Hebron. This anonymous postcard shows one of the 1923 carriages being propelled across the Afon Hwch bridge beyond Waterfall with two lucky passengers enjoying the view from the best seats on the train - the bench in the guard's compartment. (Author's Collection)

Looking the other way from the previous illustration, this time on a Peacock's tinted postcard from much earlier in the railway's life. The large station building at Hebron can just be made out, a little right of centre in the middle distance. (Author's Collection)

Passing trains at Hebron Station, on a Valentine's postcard of (probably) the 1940s or early 1950s. Note the plain nature of the sturdy station building and the replacement sleepers stacked on the old platform. (Courtesy Jan Dobrzynski)

HALFWAY

The railway's next section ends after a fairly uneventful climb on gradients of between 1 in 13 and 1 in 6, and after the railway's deepest rock cutting negotiated at the end of an S-bend some 400yd before reaching Halfway, just after the line passes the site of a tiny old slate quarry. The station is aptly named for it is situated 2 miles 23 chains (2 miles 506yd) from Llanberis and 2 miles 27 chains (2 miles 594yd) from Summit. The track gradient through the station is 1 in 11 and, at 1,641ft above sea level, the station is just over halfway up the mountain by this reckoning also.

Again there is a simple station building (added after the original wooden hut burnt down in 1910), a ground frame for operating the points of the passing loop (which is slightly longer than that at Hebron) and a watering-point. The latter is the best on the railway for as well as being supplied via a 1,000yd pipeline from a mountain stream its 9,000 gallon tank (sited 100yd up the track) is also fed via a pipeline carrying the overflow from the water tank higher up the line at Clogwyn. (The tank, like the others at the intermediate stations, is a concrete one dating back to the construction of the railway.) The present-day refreshment hut nearby is privately-owned and caters primarily for walkers.

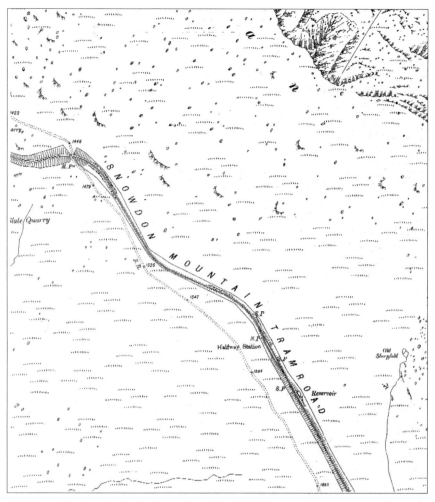

Halfway Station, as depicted on the 1900 OS 25in map. The water supply tank is clearly marked, as are the four typical intermediate station signal posts - long since removed - guarding the entrances and exits of the passing loop.

Above Hebron, the views from the railway become more and more spectacular, as this Photochrom postcard (posted 1933), looking back down the line mid-way between Hebron and Halfway, clearly shows. (Author's Collection)

Looking up the railway the views are equally impressive, as captured on this Frith's postcard of three trains passing at Halfway - with yet a fourth visible higher up the line. (Author's Collection)

Another Photochrom postcard, this time of a sight rarely seen by passengers: staff clearing snow off the track so that the essential supply trains can be kept running. (Author's Collection)

A Strathavon postcard of the former refreshment hut near Halfway Station, which catered for those making the climb on foot. Although unposted, the card bears the stamped cachet of G. Williams, Half-Way House, Snowdon, on the reverse so was presumably purchased there as a souvenir. (Author's Collection)

CLOGWYN

On the next stretch of line, from Halfway to Clogwyn, passengers notice a marked change in the nature of the railway. The scenery is now decidedly more mountainous - and becoming progressively more so - while the line itself steepens appreciably on its winding climb with long stretches at gradients of 1 in 6 or 1 in 6½ . In a boulder-strewn area known as the Valley of the Rocks, roughly mid-way along this section, is a simple platform named Rocky Valley Halt. Opened in 1974, this is where trains terminate when weather conditions are too severe for them to venture even as far as Clogwyn.

Clogwyn Station, at 3 miles 32 chains (3 miles 704yd) from Llanberis and 2,556ft above sea-level, and the only manned intermediate station on the line, is in several ways a boundary point on the railway: it marks the beginning of the final 'block section' for controlling the accident-free running of the trains over the single track, is the terminus of the railway in times of very bad weather (when either it is too windy or the track above the station is snowbound) and, not least of all, is the point where the majesty of Snowdon comes visibly into its own. Behind and below are the more mundane (by comparison) slopes and sweeps of the lower sections of the railway, ahead and above lies the rugged, exposed and breath-taking climb to Summit.

The exposed climb to Clogwyn, where the dramatic landscape comes decidedly into its own. Clogwyn Station is left of centre in the middle distance, almost directly below the mountain's peak. (Photochrom postcard, Author's Collection)

Clogwyn Station very early in the railway's life, looking towards the bend where L.A.D.A.S. left the rails on Easter Monday 1896 to disappear down the precipice on the left. Note the optical illusion of the track apparently descending beyond the station. (J. Maclardy, Oswestry)

SUMMIT

From Clogwyn, the line climbs steeper than ever with gradients as severe as 1 in 5½ - the steepest on the entire railway. A curious phenomenon connected with this can be observed from Clogwyn by looking up the line: the relatively easy gradient of 1 in 15 in the station contrasts with the preceding 1 in 6½ and the coming 1 in 5½ in such a way that the track through the station appears, quite convincingly, to slope downhill. The effect is even apparent in photographs and is produced by the changing gradients, and the actual lie of the land, giving the observer a false sense of the horizontal.

Above Clogwyn, with its incredible views down the rocky slope to the floor of the Llanberis Pass some 2,000ft below, lies the most exposed section of the line with sheer drops and craggy precipices on each side; the curve into the comparative shelter of Yr Wyddfa is the point of departure from the track, at 3 miles 66 chains (3 miles 1,452yd) from Llanberis, of *L.A.D.A.S.* on that eventful Easter Monday more than a century ago. Then it is into the last winding mile, through the cutting where the disaster originated - its rocky walls continually flaking and splintering through frost action - up the final 1 in 5½ over the skyline and into one of the two roads of Summit Station, an awesome 3,493ft above sea level. As at Llanberis, the station sports two platforms enclosing the two arrival/departure roads, but on a rather steeper 1 in 20 gradient.

From the lower terminus to the upper the railway has unrolled for a total length of 4 miles 50 chains (4 miles 1,100yd) and risen 3,140ft - an average gradient of 1 in 7.8; more statistics for the line are: over 40% of the track is curved and, besides the two great viaducts, the line has six small bridges, four of these being over paths and two over the Afon Hwch (the largest of which is an arched structure with a 50ft span).

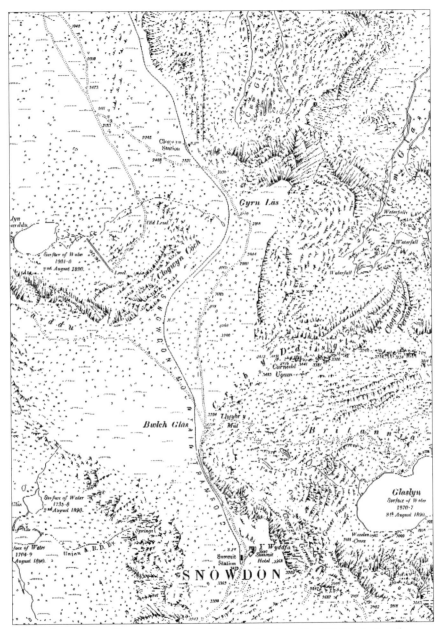

The railway from Clogwyn to Summit, as depicted on the OS 6in to 1 mile map of 1901. Although the passing loop at Clogwyn is shown, the second platform road at Summit, for some reason, is not.

The various buildings at the summit of Snowdon have had a constantly changing life. Just before the railway arrived a large wooden cabin existed here known as 'Roberts & Owens Bazaar' - an exotic name slightly out of keeping with its claim (according to the notice outside) of providing 'well aired beds, ham and eggs, and choice beverages'. This was replaced soon after the line was opened by the first Summit Hotel, completed in 1898 and staffed throughout the year. (During construction of the railway it was proposed that an observatory, complete with a powerful telescope, be erected here but the idea - though according most aptly with the railway's motto - was dropped, perhaps in recognition of the fact that weather conditions over Snowdon are not exactly ideal for star-gazing!) Intended only as a temporary building, the hotel was not replaced until 1936 when a new and rather ugly bunker-like structure was built, though since World War II overnight stayers have not been catered for, thus depriving the adventurous of the spectacle of sunrise from the summit. The building is open only during the railway's operating season; during the winter the staff depart and the premises are locked up with the windows secured with steel shutters, though these do not always prevent break-ins (usually by climbers seeking much-needed shelter after a swift change of weather). Currently, a totally new building is planned.

On a fine day the short climb to the cairn marking the very summit of the mountain produces incredible views in all directions. Immediately surrounding the peak are the spurs, ridges and cwms of the Snowdon massif, complete with their nestling lakes, beyond which can be seen the flat expanse of Anglesey and its fine dividing line of the Menai Strait. To the north are the terraced slopes of the former Dinorwic Quarries, now a silent memorial to a once great industry; to the west the long arm of the Lleyn Peninsula extending out and away from Harlech Castle; to the south, over the shoulder of Moel Hebog, can be glimpsed St David's Head marking the other limit of Cardigan Bay and, far, far beyond, on a perfect day and for those who know here to look, the distant sweep of the ocean is broken by the peaks of the Lake District, of Snaefell on the Isle of Man, and of the Wicklow Hills in Ireland.

The final approach to Summit Station, as portrayed on a Photo-Precision postcard (posted 1951), looking northwards across the coastal plain to Anglesey. (Author's Collection)

THE SUMMIT OF SNOWDON.

The original Summit Station building, and Hotel, on an anonymous postcard posted there in 1921 - hence the (faint) Summit postal cachet stamped top left. (Courtesy Jan Dobrzynski)

Stock

The Steam Locomotives: the First Design

The railway's steam locomotives fall into two distinct groups with regard to both age and design. The first group, of five locomotives, was constructed - to metric specifications - during 1895 and 1896 by the Swiss Locomotive & Machine Co of Winterthur, and followed that company's standard pattern for an Abt tank locomotive such as was already in use on several other European lines. The Snowdon engines are pure rack locomotives in that it is the rack pinions which are driven and not the wheels - the latter simply revolve freely on their axles, the first pair of which carry double rack pinions. (The third axle has no pinions and is mounted in a truck pivoted behind the second fixed axle.) All wheels are flanged.

At the very heart of the locomotive, each rack pinion has fifteen teeth around its circumference; the pair in each double pinion are a whole tooth out of step with each other while there is half a tooth's difference between the two sets to ensure the smoothest and surest total grip on the rack blades. A lubricating device also helps in this by depositing a thin film of oil upon both rack and pinions.

No	Name	Works No	Date
1	L.A.D.A.S.	923	1895
2	Enid	924	1895
3	Wyddfa	925	1895
4	Snowdon	988	1896
5	Moel Sîabod	989	1896

No 1 was destroyed in 1896.
No 4 was converted to oil-firing in 1999.

Official works photograph of No 3 Wyddfa, as built with headlamps (soon abandoned) and open cab back (later fitted with a removable window). The sloping boiler is typical of rack steam locomotives and ensures that on steep gradients the water within it remains more or less level, so protecting the firebox and steam tubes from burning through. It also gives rise to their nickname of 'kneeling cows'! (SLM Winterthur)

Close-up of the motion on one side of No 4 Snowdon, the fourth of the railway's original quintet of engines. The cylinder (directly below the nameplate) is most unusual for a steam locomotive in that the piston drives forward rather than backwards and is connected, via the vertical rocking lever on the left, to the rear driving axle - itself coupled to the front axle. (Jan Dobrzynski)

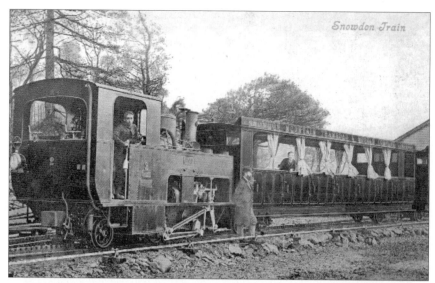

No 2 Enid *of 1895, named after Assheton-Smith's daughter, in Llanberis Station yard on a Valentine's Series postcard (the original photograph possibly having been taken at the same time as the one below). The two coaches still carry their roofboards, these being removed in the 1900s. (Author's Collection)*

No 5 Moel Sîabod *at Llanberis in 1897, this time on a one-coach train; the name is taken from the 2,860ft mountain a few miles to the east of Snowdon, just south of Capel Curig. (J. Maclardy, Oswestry)*

An unusual perspective on engine No 3 Wyddfa, emphasising the very compact design of this batch of locomotives, and the amount of space occupied by the water tanks: over 600 gallons can be carried in the tanks and boiler - still not enough for a round trip. (Jan Dobrzynski)

THE STEAM LOCOMOTIVES: THE SECOND DESIGN

The second, younger group of three steam locomotives was constructed for the railway during 1922 and 1923, again by the Swiss Locomotive & Machine Co. They are similar in their basic design to those of the first group but incorporate several improvements made in the light of the experience gained in the intervening years by both the railway and the builders, notably as regards the arrangement of the motion between the cylinders and axles. They are also fitted with steam superheating apparatus as an aid to greater efficiency, so saving some 2cwt of coal per round trip. To the casual observer the main differences in appearance are that they have different-shaped water tanks to the older engines, and false frames attached to the outside of the main, axle-supporting ones.

No	Name	Works No	Date
6	*Padarn*	2838	1922
	(Named *Sir Harmood* pre-1928)		
7	*Ralph*	2869	1923
	(Named *Aylwin* pre-1978, then *Ralph Sadler* 1978 to 1988)		
8	*Eryri*	2870	1923

Nos 7 and 8 are currently out of service.

Official work photograph of No 6 Sir Harmood (soon renamed Padarn) of 1922, the first of the second batch of locomotives built for the Snowdon Mountain Railway. (SLM Winterthur)

Official works photograph of No 8 Eryri of 1923, the last steam engine built for the railway. Both Nos 7 and 8 are almost identical to No 6, the difference being that the two younger locomotives have slightly larger water tanks. (SLM Winterthur)

BRAKING SYSTEMS

By its very nature, a rack railway imposes one all-important condition upon the design of braking systems for its stock: they must be sufficient - in theory at least - to halt a runaway train and so prevent an all too probable disaster. Conventional brakes acting on the wheels would be virtually useless and so other systems have therefore been developed for use on rack locomotives.

The Snowdon steam engines are equipped with no less than three separate braking systems, respectively hand-, steam- and air-operated, and in this follow the standard practice for steam rack locomotives. Firstly, two brake wheels in the cab can each be operated independently by either the driver or the fireman to apply half the total friction brake, which comprises eight brake shoes - four to each driving axle - bearing on a heavily-grooved steel drum each side of the double pinions; each brake wheel is connected by rodding to the four brake shoes on that side of the locomotive. Besides being a last resort in an emergency, this hand brake is used as a parking brake to hold the locomotive at a stand in the stations. The right-hand half of the friction brake also comes into effect automatically when a locomotive's speed exceeds 5mph; a centrifugal governor admits steam into a brake cylinder operating on the four brake shoes on that side of the engine.

The third braking system, known as either a counter-pressure or a compression brake, relies for its considerable power on the fact that the loco's driving pistons can be used, in reverse, to compress air; this slows down the action of the pistons and, consequently, the vehicle. In other words, the momentum of the locomotive drives the pistons instead of vice versa and in doing so the cylinders are made to work as compressors. Air is drawn into the cylinders where it is compressed, together with cooling water; the heat of the compression converts the water into steam which is allowed to escape, along with the compressed air, through a pipe behind the right-hand corner of the cab. This brake is the one used on the descent with a driver's control providing the means of regulating the rate of braking.

At the heart of the locos: a leading wheelset, previously used under No 6, on display at Llanberis Station. The double pinions (painted for clarity) are in the centre of the axle and the gear wheel for the overspeed brake is on the right. The corrugated brake drums have been removed to show the axle. (Jan Dobrzynski)

Official SIG works photograph of a 1923 coach brake bogie, supplied by SLM to the coachbuilders. (SIG Neuhausen)

THE DIESEL LOCOMOTIVES

Diesel traction was introduced on the railway in 1986 when locomotives Nos 9 and 10 entered service that summer. Built by the Hunslet Engine Co of Leeds, each is powered by a 6-cylinder 12 litre turbo-charged Rolls Royce engine producing 320hp. As with the steam locos, the mechanical drive is to the pinions and not the wheels (which again rotate freely on their coupled axles). Evolving from locomotives developed for colliery use in the 1970s, they provide a striking visual contrast to the steam locomotives whilst still giving out a reassuring impression of strength resulting from certain design features insisted upon by the railway: a distinctive 'see-through' body, an exposed engine, and rod- rather than shaft drive to the axles so as to provide a spectacle for the public akin to that of the motion on the steam engines.

Nos 9 and 10 having proved their worth, a similar pair was ordered in 1990; these likewise quickly took their places as key members of the loco fleet. Initially, the diesels did perhaps look out of place on Snowdon but, inevitably, familiarity has lessened their impact; indeed, it could be argued that in seeing them we are experiencing the same feelings as those who witnessed the arrival of the first steam locomotives on the mountain nearly a century before.

The diesels too are fitted with three braking systems: an hydraulic retarder in the transmission used on the descent, brake discs on the output shafts from the gearbox (also used as a parking brake), and an emergency brake, normally held off by the driver's constant depression of a deadman's pedal, operating on brake drums bolted to the pinions and tripped by a sensor if the axle rotates too quickly.

No	Name	Works No	Date
9	*Ninian*	9249	1986
10	*Yeti*	9250	1986
11	*Peris*	9305	1991
12	*George*	9312	1991

Diesel locomotive No 12 George in Llanberis Station in 2000; the side-on view shows clearly how its exposed engine and sturdy motion suggest its rugged strength. The name honours the former Speaker of the House of Commons, the Right Honourable George Thomas, Viscount Tonypandy. (Jan Dobrzynski)

No 12 again, leading a descending train off the Upper Viaduct in 2000. Note the excellent all-round visibility afforded the driver by the large cab windows. (Jan Dobrzynski)

THE CARRIAGES

Surprisingly, the full details of the history of the SMR's passenger stock are not known and some facts relating to the carriages are now a matter for conjecture. What is clear though is that at the time of the railway's opening the passenger fleet comprised six bogie coaches (Nos 1-6), roofed but open-sided, built by the Lancaster Railway Carriage & Wagon Co Ltd in 1895 following the then current Swiss design for rack railway carriages. Seating was for 56 passengers in seven compartments; the wooden seats were of of bare wood, arranged crosswise in the carriages and deeply concave in cross-section so as to stop passengers sliding off the rear-facing ones on the steep slopes!

In 1897 the Company decided to send one of the coaches (fleet number not known) back to Lancaster to have it converted into a fully-open vehicle; this was done, the following year, by taking off the roof and its supports and removing a two-compartment section from the centre of the body and underframes. This coach naturally afforded the best views of all - in fine weather! - especially since when it was used, in tandem with one of the closed coaches, it was marshalled at the leading end of the train. Withdrawn from service in the early 1920s when two-coach working ceased upon the arrival of more locomotives, its body either rotted away or was removed as a source of spare parts though its underframe was subsequently used as the basis for a service vehicle (see later). The five surviving 1895 coaches have all been extensively rebuilt, as detailed below, and are currently numbered 2, 3, 4, 5 and 8.

Less well documented is the railway's other open coach. Shorter in length than its companion - just four compartments - its origins are uncertain though it is believed to have arrived on the railway shortly before World War I (and possibly assigned the stock number 7). It is assumed to have been withdrawn from service at the same time as the other open coach and later underwent a similar conversion.

A two-coach train on the mountain, made up of one of the 1895 semi-open carriages and the railway's first completely open carriage, the latter vehicle the result of cutting down and shortening one of the others. (Courtesy SMR)

One of the original semi-open carriages, rebuilt and renumbered 8, at Llanberis in 2002; the number 12 on the front is a removable metal plate identifying the propelling locomotive. (Jan Dobrzynski)

In 1924 four new coaches were purchased: two to replace the withdrawn open coaches and the others to enable another two trains to be operated at peak times; their stock numbers (6-9) continued on the sequence from the remaining Lancaster coaches. They had been constructed, in 1923, by the Schweizerische Industrie-Gessellschaft of Neuhausen and were of a similar design to the Lancaster carriages, though with a few minor differences. For some reason two of these more modern coaches were withdrawn from service only a few years after their arrival on the railway and scrapped, probably in the mid-1930s; the two survivors are still in service and carry the numbers 6 and 7.

Immediately after the end of World War II a start was made on the complete modernisation of the stock, with new hardwood bodies mounted on the old underframes, at the rate of one a winter so as not to disrupt the working of the line; the work was carried out in the open on the northern platform at Llanberis Station. The rebuilt vehicles were completely enclosed with full glazing, and pull-up windows fitted to all doors, the increased wind resistance having been calculated as being well below the danger level even at the highest windspeed for which normal working was permitted. Work on the seventh and last coach was completed in 1957, after which the refurbished fleet handled all the railway's traffic for the next 30 years until, with the arrival of the diesel locos, it was decided to buy a new, fully-enclosed bogie carriage. Numbered 10, this was built for the railway by East Lancashire Coachbuilders Ltd in 1988 and seats 53 passengers. By taking full advantage of the railway's wide loading gauge it proved possible to include a central gangway plus space for wheelchair users in the new coach.

When in use, the carriages are not coupled to their propelling locomotives for safety reasons; since the entire railway is built on an uphill slope, a carriage always remains in contact with the locomotive behind it and cannot therefore run away - or indeed be dragged away if the locomotive should suffer any mishap. Like the engines, they too are fitted with double pinions in contact with the rack blades, and with both manual and automatic brakes.

Official SIG works photograph of the interior of one of the 1923 carriages, looking towards the guard's compartment. (SIG Neuhausen)

Official SLM photograph of the guard's compartment end of a 1923 carriage loaded ready for its journey by rail across Europe to Wales. (Courtesy SMR)

Coach No 7, one of the railway's two surviving (rebuilt) 1923 carriages, captured in Llanberis yard in 2000. (Jan Dobrzynski)

The railway's youngest coach is carriage No 10 of 1988, seen here at Llanberis in 2000 next to the rebuilt and renumbered No 8 of 1895. (Jan Dobrzynski)

The Railcars

In 1995 the railway took delivery of three diesel-electric railcars constructed by HPE Tredegar Ltd of Tredegar in South Wales. All three vehicles are identical and can be operated as single units or coupled together to form a two- or three-unit train; each railcar seats 41 passengers and, like carriage No 10, can accommodate wheelchair users. Each vehicle has a cab at each end; when one is working as a single unit it is manned by a driver in the leading (forward-facing) cab, plus a guard; when two or more are operated a multiple-unit the same crew of two is used, the driver occupying the leading cab of the train.

Each railcar is equipped with a 8.3 litre 184hp diesel engine driving an alternator unit generating 440V of electrical power, the current in turn powering a 3-phase AC traction motor connected to an axle-hung, final-drive gearbox driving a pair of pinions. Four braking systems are fitted: regenerative (ie allowing the pinions to drive the motor so converting it into a dynamo, the effort involved thus slowing the pinions); air-brake; emergency rack brake and an automatic overspeed brake (plus a deadman's pedal).

No	Works No	Date
21	1074	1995
22	1075	1995
23	1076	995

Two of the railway's three new railcars at work, running as a multiple-unit across the Afon Hwch outside Llanberis Station in 2000. (Jan Dobrzynski)

THE GOODS STOCK

In addition to its passenger carriages, the SMR has always operated a small number of goods or service vehicles. In the beginning the hope was that freight could be carried to and from farms on the lower slopes of the mountain, hence the provision of goods sidings at the first three stations. To this end the Lancaster Carriage & Wagon Co supplied four small, drop-sided wagons (Nos 1-4) to the railway in 1895 along with the coaches; the hoped-for goods traffic never materialised however and three of the wagons were left to rot quietly away while just one was kept in good repair for carrying supplies to the Summit Hotel.

The railway's only other goods vehicle currently in service was produced by mounting a 1 ton capacity fuel bunker and a 700 gallon water tank on the underframe of the withdrawn 1895 open coach described earlier. After World War II a basic caboose-type body (since rebuilt) was added to protect the brakeman, and the old water tank discarded and a removable, 400 gallon one substituted. Officially numbered 1, it is used in conjunction with the surviving low wagon to form the service train propelled up the line by one of the locos each day ferrying supplies to Summit Station. (It is also employed to carry staff, tools and materials to wherever track or other maintenance work is being carried out.)

The railway's only other goods vehicle was - probably - constructed from the withdrawn four-compartment open coach mentioned earlier. Stripped of its body, this was used during World War II to carry coal, coke and fuel oil to the busy summit complex, after which it was scrapped.

Two of the railway's original low wagons - half the then goods stock - in the care of locomotive No 3 Wyddfa at Llanberis, possibly even before the railway opened. (Author's Collection)

The essential service train at Summit Station, probably in the 1950s or 1960s. Locomotive No 5 Moel Sîabod waits to take it back down the mountain, the railway's sole surviving low wagon laden with rubbish from the summit complex. (Courtesy Lens of Sutton)

THE RAILWAY IN COLOUR

The Snowdon Mountain Railway is nothing if not colourful, with its brightly-painted locomotives, railcars and cariages - not to mention the eye-catching Llanberis Station complex itself offering the first glimpse of the railway for most visitors to the line.

Accounts of the locomotives' early livery vary widely but, as far as can be ascertained, it appears to have been a plain, dark mahogany red that was almost a chocolate brown (the same colour in fact as the carriages). This was later changed to black, again unlined, during World War II before a post-war colour scheme of apple green, black and red was arrived at. Bodywork lining was also bright red. This livery lasted until the mid-1990s when it was decided to paint each locomotive (including the diesels) a different colour - a departure from 'normal' railway practice but an idea increasingly adopted by preserved railways so as to make their loco fleets more interesting to the general public.

The livery carried by the SMR's carriages has also changed over the years, with different colour schemes often overlapping. The original vehicles were an unlined chocolate brown, with the new 1920s coaches cherry red with a thin white lining. During World War II all were painted plain grey as an austerity measure, with this later replaced for a few years by all-over green to match the locomotives. With the rebuilds from 1951 onwards a new livery of unlined cherry red was used with the present colours adopted after the conversions were completed: unlined cherry red for the lower panels, cream for the upper bodywork and grey for the roofs. Running gear is thought to have always been black.

The goods wagons were originally grey, lettered in white.

It is hoped that the following selection of images, old and new, will give a taste of the railway in its full glory.

Snowdon. Tram at Clogwyn Coch.

Snowdon. Tram between Clogwyn and Summit.

Snowdon. Tram at 1st Viaduct.

Snowdon. Tram crossing 1st Viaduct.

A Peacock "AUTOCHROM" multi-view postcard, posted 1936 but originally produced much earlier, of the SMR. Cards of this type were very popular as souvenirs since the buyer was getting several pictures for the price of one! (Author's Collection)

An early Valentine's postcard of a train crossing the Upper Viaduct, with part of Llyn Padarn and the Dinorwic Quarries in the background. (Courtesy Jan Dobrzynski)

An LNWR official-issue postcard, posted 1911, of a two-coach train on the Upper Viaduct. The practice of running two carriages together became obsolete with the arrival of extra stock in the 1920s. (Author's Collection)

An early Grosvenor Series postcard of a train just below Clogwyn, with a second train visible in the distance. (Author's Collection)

Another Peacock "AUTOCHROM" postcard, this time of locomotive No 4 Snowdon in Clogwyn Station - probably waiting for the descending train to pass. (Author's Collection)

A J. Salmon of Sevenoaks postcard, posted 1947, of the final approach to Summit, showing clearly the hostile nature of the terrain encountered by the railway's constructors. (Author's Collection)

Another Grosvenor Series postcard, posted 1907, of the summit of the mountain and its original Hotel and Station buildings, and the signals - removed in the 1920s - originally installed to control train movements in and out of the terminus. (Author's Collection)

A Peacock "AUTOCHROM" postcard, posted 1906, of Summit Station, with No 4 Snowdon *on a train again. (Author's Collection)*

SNOWDON SUMMIT. IN WINTER.
L. & N.W. RAILWAY.

An LNWR official-issue postcard, posted 1909, giving a somewhat romanticised view of the summit of Snowdon in winter. (Author's Collection)

Llanberis Station, as approached from the village, in 2000; the imposing white building is the Royal Victoria Hotel, for many years intimately bound-up with the fortunes of the railway. (Author)

Llanberis Station entrance, with the original wooden building (right) and stone office block (left) much added to and extended over the years. (Author)

Llanberis Station from the tracks, 2000. The building nearest the camera is the nerve-centre for the daily operation of the railway, the Traffic Control Office. (Author)

Looking into the station yard at Llanberis, again in 2000, with locomotives No 2 in blue livery and No 5 in black. (Author)

In the station yard at Llanberis, looking back to the Traffic Control Office, 2000, with No 5 simmering quietly by the coaling stage. (Author)

Spare boilers in Llanberis yard, visible evidence of the railway's unceasing maintenance programme necessitated by the enormous demands made on the locomotives. (Author)

Above Hebron, the sheer immensity of the scenery can make a train seen very insignificant indeed, as here in 2000... (Author)

... though anyone taking the footpath from Llanberis has the ideal vantage point to see both at their best... (Author)

... especially when the weather is glorious, as here in 2001... (Jan Dobrzynski)

... or here, the same day, with spectacular vistas opening up all around on the final approach... (Jan Dobrzynski)

... to the summit. (Jan Dobrzynski)

Sometimes, though, the view at the top is not so impressive - or even non-existent - as on this misty day in 2000. (Author)

Steam locomotive No 5's name and number plates, as displayed in 2000 - the numeral has been moved from its original position on the side of the cab to below the name. (Author)

A Hunslet works plate now carried by No 4 Snowdon, denoting its 1963 rebuild in Leeds. (Author)

Steam locomotive number and works plates, as carried by No 4 Snowdon. (Author)

A rear view of No 12, showing details of its livery - which differ between the diesels - and the common arrangement of numbers, name and works plates on the cab sides and back. (Author)

Two of the railway's three new railcars in operation in 2000, crossing the Afon Hwch outside Llanberis Station on their way, as multipule-unit, to Summit.The livery is that currently used for the other passenger vehicles, but with added green. (Author)

The passenger stock's current livery of plain red and cream, sported here in 2000 by carriage No 7, one of the rebuilt 1923 vehicles, with purple-liveried George, at the foot of the Afon Hwch Viaduct. (Author)

The red and cream livery extends to the caboose, seen here at Llanberis in one of the new carriage sidings, also in 2000; the other half of the service train, the flat wagon, sports its old grey however. (Author)

94

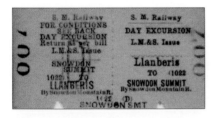 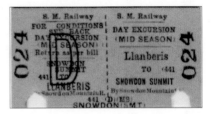

Finally, a selection of special tickets used on the SMR over the years, including two excursion tickets issued by other operators and one commemorating Queen Elizabeth II's Silver Jubilee.

Other titles in the series by Keith Turner:

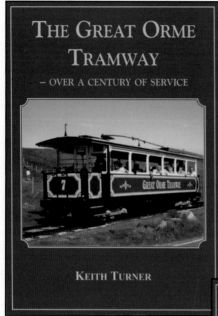

For over 100 years, the Great Orme Tramway has served faithfully the northern Wales seaside resort of Llandudno.

£5.50

One of the last tramways to operate – fond memories of the service between Llandudno and Colwyn Bay.

£5.50

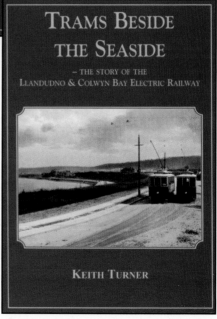